D1072070

South Africa

by Lucia Raatma

Content Adviser: Professor Sherry L. Field,
Department of Social Science Education, College of Education,
The University of Georgia

Reading Adviser: Dr. Linda D. Labbo,
Department of Reading Education, College of Education,
The University of Georgia

COMPASS POINT BOOKS

Minneapolis, Minnesota

FIRST REPORTS

Compass Point Books
3722 West 50th Street, #115
Minneapolis, MN 55410

Visit Compass Point Books on the Internet at *www.compasspointbooks.com* or e-mail your request to *custserv@compasspointbooks.com*.

Cover: Camps Bay in Cape Peninsula, South Africa

Photographs ©: Joe Viesti/Viesti Collection Inc., cover; Photo Network/Chad Ehlers, 4, 12; Photo Network/Christine Pemberton, 5; Steve McCutcheon/Visuals Unlimited, 6, 37; TRIP/J. Farmar, 8; Jason Laure, 9, 10, 11, 13, 14, 30, 33, 35, 36, 41, 42; Doug Sokell/Visuals Unlimited, 15; Gil Lopez-Espina/Visuals Unlimited, 16, 17; Brian Rogers/Visuals Unlimited, 18; Hulton Getty/ Archive Photos, 19, 20, 25, 29, 32; Stock Montage, 21; James Alan Brown/Visuals Unlimited, 22, 28, 34; North Wind Picture Archives, 23, 24, 26, 27; Ulli Michel/Hulton Getty/Archive Photos, 31; TRIP/S. Harris, 38; TRIP/F. Salgado, 39 top; Juda Ngwenya/Hulton Getty/Archive Photos, 39 bottom; Greta Pratt/Hulton Getty/Archive Photos, 40; Jessie M. Harris, 43; Norman Owen Tomalin/ Bruce Coleman Inc., 45.

Editors: E. Russell Primm, Emily J. Dolbear, and Neal Durando
Photo Researcher: Svetlana Zhurkina
Photo Selector: Catherine Neitge
Designer: Bradfordesign, Inc.

Library of Congress Cataloging-in-Publication Data

Raatma, Lucia.
    South Africa / by Lucia Raatma.
       p. cm. — (First reports)
    Includes bibliographical references and index.
    ISBN 0-7565-0131-8 (lib bdg)
    1. South Africa—Juvenile literature. [1. South Africa.] I. Title. II. Series.
    DT1719 .R33 2000
    968—dc21   2001001459

Table of Contents

▲ *Costumed dancers perform in Cape Town.*

"Sawubona!"

If you visit South Africa, you may be greeted by a friendly "*Sawubona!*" This Zulu word means "Good morning, good afternoon, and good night." Zulu is one of many languages spoken in South Africa.

As its name says, South Africa is the southernmost country on the **continent** of Africa. To the east and

▲ *Table Mountain is a famous landmark in Cape Town.*

▲ *The city of Pretoria*

south is the Indian Ocean. To the west is the Atlantic Ocean.

Five countries border South Africa on the north. They are Namibia, Botswana, Zimbabwe, Mozambique, and Swaziland.

South Africa has nine **provinces**. The country has three capitals—one for each branch of the government. Bloemfontein, Cape Town, and Pretoria are the capital cities.

NAMIBIA

ZIMBABWE

BOTSWANA

MOZAMBIQUE

Limpopo

Kruger
Nat'l
Park

Pietersburg ★

Kwazulu Natal

Pretoria ⊛

Nelspruit
★

Johannesburg ★

**Eastern
Transvaal**

Mafikeng ★

Gauteng

SWAZILAND

North West

Vaal

Free State

Orange

Kimberley ★

Bloemfontein ⊛

Ulundi
★

**Kwazulu
Natal**

LESOTHO

**Northern
Cape**

S O U T H

A F R I C A

Orange

Durban ●

D R A K E N S B E R G   M T S.

ATLANTIC
OCEAN

INDIAN
OCEAN

**Eastern
Cape**

Bisho ★

**Western
Cape**

Cape Town ⊛

● Port Elizabeth

N
W ✦ E
S

0   150   300 miles

0   150   300 kilometers

▲ *Map of South Africa*

A Rugged Land

South Africa has many kinds of land. **Plateaus** cover about two-thirds of the country. The three main ones are the Highveld, the Middleveld, and the Bushveld.

The highest mountains in South Africa are the Drakensberg Mountains. Champagne Castle is the

▲ *The Drakensberg Mountains*

highest point. It snows in South Africa, but only in the mountains.

The longest river is the Orange. It flows to the Atlantic Ocean. It is also part of South Africa's border with Namibia.

Other important rivers are the Vaal and the Limpopo. Many of South Africa's rivers are dry for

▲ *The Limpopo River*

▲ *A lighthouse marks the high point at the Cape of Good Hope.*

most of the year. Dams have been built to provide water all year.

The coast of South Africa has sharp cliffs. There are a number of ports along the coast. One of the most important is Saldanha Bay in the southwest. Other ports are Durban and Cape Town.

Using the Land

On much of the land in the Highveld, farmers raise cattle and grow corn. The Middleveld is very dry. Only sheep are raised here.

The Bushveld gets more rain than anywhere else in South Africa. Farmers there grow citrus and other fruits.

▲ *A sheep farm*

▲ *Grapes are harvested to make wine.*

South Africa produces more gold than any other country. Diamonds are also found in some mines. These are important **resources**. Other mines produce uranium, platinum, and coal.

▲ *A gold miner drills a hole.*

Plants and Animals

▲ *A wide variety of wildflowers blooms in South Africa.*

The plateaus are covered mostly in grasses. Trees and bushes grow in the north. Fields of flowers bloom in spring rains on the Northern Cape.

On the coast, yellowwood, ironwood, and lemonwood trees grow. There are also some areas of **rain forest**.

▲ *Ironwood tree*

Lions, elephants, antelopes, monkeys, zebras, and leopards all live in South Africa. These animals are now found only in **preserves**.

▲ *Elephants live in preserves in South Africa.*

▲ *Zebras take a drink in Kruger National Park.*

Kruger National Park is known for its South African animals. It is also home to a herd of black rhinoceroses. Only a few black rhinoceroses are left in the world today.

Snakes live all over South Africa. You can also find quail, pheasant, and ostriches.

Most of South Africa is warm for much of the year. Usually there is little rain. Sometimes it rains hard enough to cause flooding, however.

▲ *It is usually dry in South Africa.*

The Early People of South Africa

Long ago, South Africans hunted animals and gathered food to eat. These people were called the Khoikhoi.

The Bantu were another group of people who lived in early South Africa. They raised animals.

▲ *A Khoikhoi tribesman drinks from an ostrich egg used as a bottle.*

▲ *An 1878 illustration of a young Bantu chief*

The Bantu forced out many of the Khoikhoi. Those who remained joined the Bantu.

In 1652, Dutch settlers arrived in South Africa. They lived apart from the Bantu.

French and German people soon joined the Dutch. These European people were called Afrikaners or Boers. *Boer* is a Dutch word meaning "farmer."

The Afrikaners farmed the land and raised cattle. They brought slaves from Asia and other parts of Africa to work on their farms.

▲ *Slaves worked on the farms.*

Soon the Europeans and the Bantu began to fight over the land. Many of the Bantu left South Africa. Those who stayed behind split into new groups. They were the Swazi, Sotho, and Zulu.

Struggles for Land

The leader of the Zulu was named Shaka. He was a very good general. Shaka invented new ways to fight. He gave his warriors the *assengai*, a spear with a very long blade.

▲ *Traditional Zulu houses*

Shaka was smart, but he was also very cruel. He ruled much of South Africa until he was killed by his half brothers.

British settlers arrived in the early 1800s. They made the people of what was then called Cape Colony follow English laws. They even made English the official language.

These changes angered the Afrikaners. Many Afrikaner families left Cape Colony. They moved to other parts of South Africa.

▲ *Many Afrikaner families moved away from Cape Colony, as shown in this 1850 woodcut.*

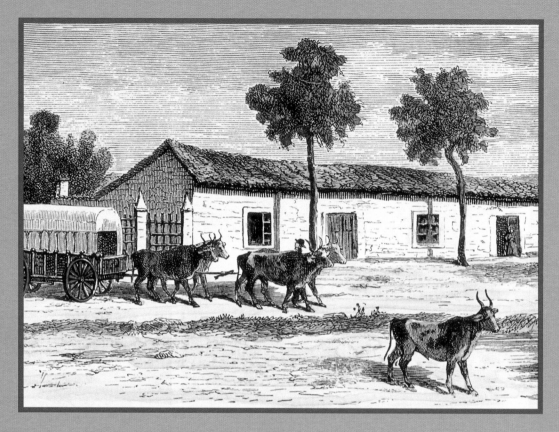

▲ *A Boer farm*

As the Afrikaners moved across the land, they met the Xhosa. The Xhosa were related to the Bantu people. The Afrikaners and the Xhosa fought over land.

Soon the British began to fight the Xhosa too. In the end, the Xhosa were beaten. All their land became part of Cape Colony.

This was not the last war in South Africa. Gold was discovered near Johannesburg in 1886. The Afrikaners controlled this area, but the British wanted to mine the gold. Afrikaner leader Paul Kruger tried to stop the British.

▲ *African and European miners searched for gold in the 1880s.*

The Afrikaners tried to fight the British for more than two years. But the British forces outnumbered them. This conflict is called the Boer War.

During the war, the British destroyed Afrikaner farms. Many Afrikaners died in prison. In the end, the Transvaal became a British colony.

▲ *Afrikaners attacked the British in 1902.*

Becoming a Republic

In 1910, the British joined their four colonies—Cape Colony, Natal, Transvaal, and the Orange Free State—into one country. They called it the Union of South Africa.

The country was made a **republic** in 1961. Many years would pass before all South Africans would be free.

▲ *A village in the Orange Free State*

South Africans Today

▲ *Zulu women return from the market in the ZwaZulu/Natal province.*

Most South Africans are black. The next largest group is white. The Asians and the Coloreds are the other main groups in South Africa. The Coloreds are people of mixed race.

In spite of the many blacks in South Africa, an unfair system called **apartheid** lasted for many years there. Apartheid was a law that

▲ *A Bantu woman shopping in the Durban Indian market in 1948,*
the year apartheid became law

▲ *A photo shop took pictures needed for passbooks, which blacks had to carry at all times.*

gave all the power to white people. The whites controlled the government. They made most of the decisions for the country.

▲ *F. W. de Klerk, left, and Nelson Mandela*

One of the men who fought apartheid was Nelson Mandela. He was kept in prison on Robben Island for twenty-seven years. Nelson Mandela helped people see that apartheid was wrong.

In 1990, President F. W. de Klerk released Mandela from jail. These two men won the Nobel Peace Prize in 1993 for ending apartheid.

▲ *In 1994, Nelson Mandela cast his ballot in the first election in South Africa in which people of all races could vote.*

In 1994, Nelson Mandela was elected president of South Africa. He served until 1999.

Life in South Africa

▲ Signs in Afrikaans

In the past, South Africa had only two official languages. They were English and Afrikaans, the language of the Afrikaners. Many blacks, Coloreds, and Asians spoke their own languages.

After apartheid ended, the government added

▲ *These women and children speak Venda, one of South Africa's eleven official languages.*

nine official languages. They were Zulu, Xhosa, Tswana, Venda, Tsonga, Ndebele, Swazi, Northern Sotho, and Southern Sotho. South Africa now has

▲ *Schoolchildren in Cape Town*

eleven official languages. Most people speak two or more languages.

For many years, blacks and whites had to attend separate schools. Now all schools are open to all people. More schools must be built, however.

The largest cities in South Africa are Cape Town, Johannesburg, Pretoria, and Port Elizabeth. Durban is the country's leading port.

Soweto is the name of a township outside Johannesburg. A township was a place where only black people lived. It was against the law for them to live in the city.

▲ *Soweto is a huge township near Johannesburg.*

▲ *A Dutch Reform Church in Swellendam*

Most South Africans are Christians. But there are also many Hindus, Muslims, and Jews. Many South Africans believe in a god and in the power of spirits.

▲ *A rugby match in Durban*

South Africans enjoy many sports such as tennis, golf, and cricket. Soccer and rugby are popular too.

The Arts and Beyond

▲ *Murals cover the walls of Soweto.*

South Africans express themselves in many forms of art. Township art is a style of painting that expresses the country's struggle with apartheid.

South Africa has many fine writers. Nadine Gordimer won the Nobel Prize for literature in 1991.

◄ *Archbishop Desmond Tutu, who won a Nobel Prize for his anti-apartheid work, and Nobel Prize–winning author Nadine Gordimer*

39

Breyten Breytenbach has written many poems against apartheid.

South African music has been influenced by many cultures. For example, Ladysmith Black Mambazo is a group that sings in a Zulu style. They became famous around the world by playing with the American singer Paul Simon.

▲ *Paul Simon, right, performs with Ladysmith Black Mambazo.*

▲ *In some South African families, nannies care for children and live with the families.*

South Africa has worked hard to make changes since apartheid. Some things are very slow to improve, however. Whites still have more money than blacks, Coloreds, and Asians. Women are not treated as well as men are.

▲ *Yachts race in the Atlantic Ocean with Table Mountain in the background.*

South Africans have much to look forward to. Tourists come from all over the world to visit South Africa. Little by little, things are getting better for all South Africans. "*Sizobonana*!" That's how the Zulus say "So long! Hope to see you again soon."

▲ *South Africa's children hope for a bright future.*

Glossary

apartheid—the separation of people of different races

continent—one of Earth's seven great landmasses

plateaus—high, flat land areas

preserves—areas set aside to protect plants and animals

provinces—districts within some countries

rain forest—a dense tropical forest where a lot of rain falls

republic—a country in which the people elect their leaders

resources—the natural wealth of a country

Did You Know?

• Almost half of the people of South Africa live in cities.

• South Africa has twenty daily newspapers.

• South Africa has more than 2 million cellular phones in use.

• In the 1960s, Stephen Biko started a movement in South Africa based on the Black Power movement in the United States. He was killed by the police in 1977.

At a Glance

Official name: Republic of South Africa

Capitals: Pretoria (administrative), Cape Town (legislative), and Bloemfontein (judicial)

Official languages: English, Afrikaans, and nine African languages

National anthems: "Die Stem van Suid-Africa" ("The Call of South Africa"); "Nkosi Sikelel' iAfrika" ("God Bless Africa")

Area: 471,445 square miles (1,221,043 square kilometers)

Highest point: Champagne Castle, 11,072 feet (3,377 meters)

Lowest point: Sea level

Population: 46,215,000 (2000 estimate)

Head of government: President

Money: Rand

Important Dates

A.D. 100	Bantu people enter South Africa from the north.
1652	Dutch settlers arrive in Cape Town.
1867	Diamonds are discovered near Kimberley.
1886	Gold is discovered near Johannesburg.
1893	Mahatma Gandhi begins working for Indian rights in South Africa.
1910	The Union of South Africa is formed.
1948	Apartheid begins.
1961	South Africa becomes a republic.
1989	F. W. de Klerk becomes president.
1990	Nelson Mandela is freed from prison.
1991	Apartheid ends.
1994	Mandela is elected president.

What to Know More?

At the Library

Cooper, Floyd. *Mandela: From the Life of the South African Statesman.* New York: Puffin, 2000.

Dahl, Michael S. *South Africa.* Mankato, Minn.: Bridgestone Books, 1998.

Green, Jen. *A Family from South Africa.* Austin, Tex.: Raintree/Steck-Vaughn, 1998.

Holland, Gini. *Nelson Mandela.* Austin, Tex.: Raintree/Steck-Vaughn, 1997.

On the Web
South Africa National Parks
http://www.parks-sa.co.za/
For descriptions of parks throughout the country

South Africa Online
http://www.southafrica.co.za/
For a guide to travel, business, and lifestyles

Through the Mail
South African Embassy
3051 Massachusetts Avenue, N.W.
Washington, DC 20008
To get information about the country

On the Road
National Museum of African Art
950 Independence Avenue, S.W.
Washington, DC 20001
202/357-4600
To tour a branch of the Smithsonian Institution devoted to African art

About the Author

Lucia Raatma received her bachelor's degree in English literature from the University of South Carolina and her master's degree in cinema studies from New York University. She has written a wide range of books for young people. When she is not researching or writing, she enjoys going to movies, playing tennis, practicing yoga, and spending time with her husband, daughter, and golden retriever. She lives in New York.

Bluegill
Lepomis macrochirus Rafinesque

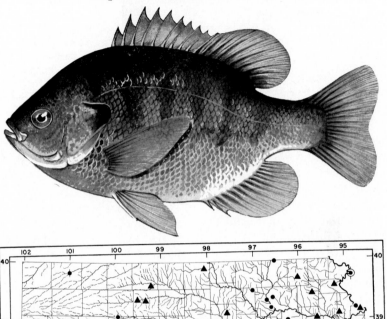

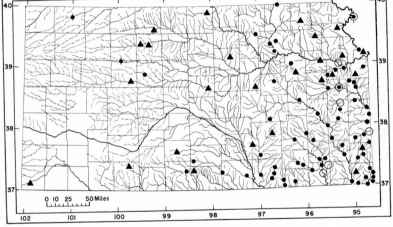

Pomotis luna, Snow (1875:140-141); Wheeler (1879:33).

Lepomis pallidus, Jordan and Meek (1885:14); Graham (1885b:76); Dyche (1914:63, 115).

Helioperca incisor, Hall (1934:231).

Lepomis macrochirus, Breukelman (1940a:374, 1940b:382, 384, 1960:12, 34); Jennings (1942:366); Greer and Cross (1956:360); Schelske (1957:48); Clarke, Breukelman, and Andrews (1958:169); Cross, Deacon, and Ward (1959:163-164); Metcalf (1959:382, 1966:157); Minckley (1959:429); Deacon (1961:399); Deacon and Metcalf (1961: 318); Hastings and Cross (1962:10, 15-16); Fisher (1962:428); Kilgore and Rising (1965:142).

Lepomis machrochirus, Maupin, Wells, and Leist (1954:168, 171).

Lepomis macrochirus macrochirus, Cross (1954:312).

Bluegill—Schoonover and Thompson (1954:174).

Body compressed, rounded; mouth small and oblique; dorsal fin with 10 high spines, 11 or 12 soft-rays; anal fin with 3 spines, 10 or 11 rays; pelvic fin with 1 spine, 5 rays; pectoral fin long, acutely pointed, with 13 rays; lateral line complete, arched anteriorly, with 41-45 scales; opercular flap short, flexible, dark to its margin; gill rakers slender; vertebrae usually 29.

Adults greenish or gray dorsally, silvery laterally; juveniles having 9-12 distinct vertical bars, evenly spaced on pale background. Breeding males dark, olivaceous to bronze, breast orange; fins densely pigmented, pelvics and anal almost black but overlain by bluish iridescence; dorsal fin with dark basal blotch posteriorly.

Largest Kansas bluegill 11 inches long, weight 2 pounds 5 ounces [Kansas Fish and Game 23(1):11, 15. 1966].

Judging from the scarcity of early records, the bluegill was uncommon, and was confined to eastern streams, when settlement began in Kansas. The accounts of Snow, Wheeler, Jordan and Meek, and Graham indicate that bluegills occurred in Kansas a century ago, but their absence from collections reported by Gilbert, Cragin, Hay, Evermann and Fordice, and Jordan is suggestive of a restricted distribution. All specimens that are extant in collections made prior to 1913 by personnel of the State Biological Survey were obtained east of 96° longitude. The State Fish Hatchery at Pratt had been established by that time, however, and bluegills were being propagated there; Dyche (1914:63) wrote that bluegills were then "found in some Kansas streams and should be introduced into all of them. . . . No fish does better in ponds at the State Hatchery."

The construction of almost 100,000 farm ponds in the past half-century, and advocacy of the bluegill as a pondfish by conservation agencies, brought about rapid westward extension of the range of this species. The map above fails to reflect the widespread distribution of bluegills, because farm ponds are not represented among the locality-records shown. *L. macrochirus* remains scarce in western streams owing to their generally shallow, sandy channels, but the species may be found almost anywhere in Kansas as the result of escapement from farm ponds.

The popularity of the bluegill stems from its excellence as a sport-fish and its suitability as forage for bass in clear ponds. On the other hand, bluegills are inherently small fishes that attain sizes large enough to interest anglers only when they are subject to heavy predation—in ponds having high populations of bass or other large piscivorous fishes. Data obtained in 1951 and 1952 from three ponds on the Floyd T. Amsden farm in Barber County exemplify the important variability in growth-rate of this species. In one of the ponds, bluegills required seven years to reach an average length of six inches and weight of three ounces. So few of the fish in this pond were "keepers" that its value for angling was negligible, despite the dense population of fish that existed there. Bluegills in a second pond on this farm attained a length of seven inches, and weight of four to five ounces, when three years old. This rate of growth is fast enough to provide satisfactory angling, but few of the fish in that pond weighed more than five ounces. Sixty of the four- to five-ounce fish were transferred in July, 1951, to a third pond, about one acre in size, that lacked bluegills. When fourteen of these bluegills were caught in June of the following year, they weighed seven to twelve ounces (average 9½ ounces). Relieved of competition, these fish gained more weight in a few months than they had gained in their first three years of life. Their average gain after transfer greatly exceeded the individual weights attained in seven years by bluegills in the first pond.

"Stunting" like that described for the first pond above is usual in muddy ponds, and is frequent in clear ponds that have extensive areas of shallow water overgrown by aquatic vegetation. Neither of these two kinds of ponds will sustain satisfactory angling-success for bluegills. The species should be used only in ponds having clear water and steep shorelines; and, of course, predaceous species should be stocked with the bluegills.

Reproduction by bluegills extends from April to September, but most spawning takes place in May or June, when water-temperatures exceed 68° F. The males make individual nests, usually near shore where the water is one to four feet deep, over almost any kind of substrate (mud, sand or gravel, vegetation). The nest is a saucerlike depression, which the male forms by vigorous caudal fanning-movements that remove silt from the bottom. The diameter of the nest usually is at least nine to ten inches, or approximately twice the length of the attendant fish. Each male hovers above its nest, or swims rapidly along the circular margin of the nest, driving away intruders. The individual territories are small. Nests are sometimes adjacent, separated only by a narrow ridge, and are concentrated along limited segments of the shoreline.

Females are admitted into the nest when ready to deposit eggs, which are fertilized by the male as they are extruded onto the floor of the nest; the eggs adhere to objects on the substrate during their development. The female leaves the nest-area after spawning, but may return at a later time to deposit additional eggs in the same nest or a different one. After hatching, the fry remain in or near the nest for several days before departing finally from the protective influence of the guardian male. Subsequently, the young occupy shallow water alongshore, or dense beds of vegetation, where they are partly sheltered from predation. Bluegills are gregarious, usually occurring in loose aggregations throughout life.

The food of bluegills consists mainly of small crustaceans and insects. The amount of food available, in relation to the abundance of bluegills, strongly influences their rate of growth. Few bluegills live longer than four or five years in Kansas, so angling-success for bluegills is poor unless they attain a length of six inches before their fourth year of life.

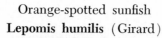

Orange-spotted sunfish
Lepomis humilis (Girard)

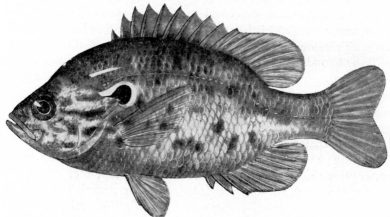

Lepomis anagallinus Cope (1869:221 [orig. descr.]).
Lepiopomus anagallinus, Jordan (1877a:35).
Lepomis humilis, Gilbert (1884:16, 1885b:99, 1886:211, 1889:39, 40); Cragin (1885b:110); Graham (1885a:4, 1885b:75); Evermann and Fordice (1886:186); Hay (1887:243, 247, 250, 252); Jordan (1891:18); Breukelman (1940a:374, 1940b:382, 1960:12, 34); Jennings (1942: 366); Cross (1954:312); Moore and Buck (1955:26); Minckley (1956: 355); Greer and Cross (1956:361); Schelske (1957:48); Clarke, Breukelman, and Andrews (1958:169); Minckley and Cross (1959:212); Metcalf (1959:381-382, 1966:156); Minckley (1959:429); Deacon (1961:398-399); Deacon and Metcalf (1961:318); Hastings and Cross (1962:10); Fisher (1962:428); Kilgore and Rising (1965:142).
Allotis humilis, Hall (1934:231).

Body compressed; dorsal fin with 10 or 11 spines, 9 or 10 soft-rays; anal fin with 3 spines, 8 or 9 soft-rays; pelvics with 1 spine, 5 soft-rays; pectorals with 12-14 rays; lateral line complete or incomplete (often irregularly inter-

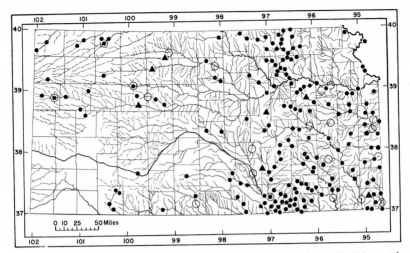

rupted), arched anteriorly, with 34-39 scales; opercular flap flexible, with rounded central dark spot and broad white margin; gill rakers slender, not knoblike; lateral-line canals on head conspicuously enlarged (unique to this species of *Lepomis*); vertebrae 29.

Olivaceous dorsally, sides greenish silver with scattered reddish-brown dots; young having few widely-spaced vertical bars on sides; breeding males with bright orange lateral spots; sides of head iridescent pale-blue, streaked by bright orange; breast and belly orange; fins brilliantly orange, pelvics and anal narrowly outlined by black; iris red or orange. See Plate 3.

Length approximately four inches.

The orange-spotted sunfish occurs throughout Kansas, rivaling the green sunfish in ubiquity and abundance. The species never grows large enough to qualify as a sport-fish, except as it may excite an occasional tad who catches one on a worm-baited No. 12 hook. In contrast to the more highly-regarded basses, crappies, and bluegill, the distribution of the orangespot probably has not changed as a result of lake-construction and stocking-programs. Early records demonstrate its widespread occurrence in Kansas at the time of settlement. As Metcalf (1966:157) suggested, *L. humilis* probably originated in the Ancestral Plains Drainage, and spread eastward and northward as segments of that basin were captured by western tributaries of the Mississippi System.

The orangespot sometimes gains access to lakes and ponds, but is seldom so prevalent there as the green sunfish. *L. humilis* mainly inhabits pools in small streams, often in company with green sunfish and, in southeastern Kansas, with long-eared sunfish. The general abundance of orangespots obscures their habitat-preference. They seem indifferent to bottom-type—rocky, sandy, or muddy; they tolerate high turbidity and extensive fluctuation in waterlevel. I think, though, that L. humilis is best adapted to sandy streams, whereas green sunfish prevail in creeks having mud- or shale-bottoms, and longears definitely prefer the rocky bottom and clear water of streams that course across exposed limestone-strata in eastern Kansas.

Like other species of Lepomis, the orangespot has a lengthy reproductive season, extending throughout the warm months (water-temperature 75° to 89° F.), but reaching a peak in late May and June. The spawning-habits are generally like those of the bluegill. Nests are often in colonies, where the males defend individual territories only a foot or two in diameter. When frightened off their nests, several males may move together into deep water before returning, seconds later, to their respective breeding-territories. Most nests of orangespots that I have seen were situated where sand or fine gravel could be exposed, as the floor of the nest, by the fanning-away of a thin layer of sediment. The depth of water over nests varied from four inches to two feet. The eggs are minute and nearly colorless, having the appearance of clear quartz sand. The eggs adhere to sand-grains on the floor of the nest and are highly vulnerable to certain minnows that are commonly associated with orange-spotted sunfish; red shiners, for example, will instantly swarm into nests to devour the eggs if they are deserted momentarily by the guardian male orangespot.

Where abundant, L. humilis is a significant forage-item for larger centrarchids. Probably it is also competitive for food with young bass, bluegill, and crappies.

Longear

Lepomis megalotis (Rafinesque)

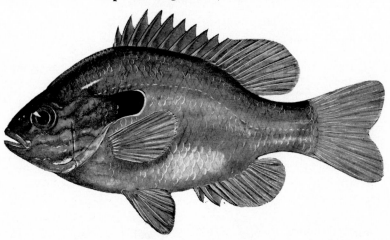

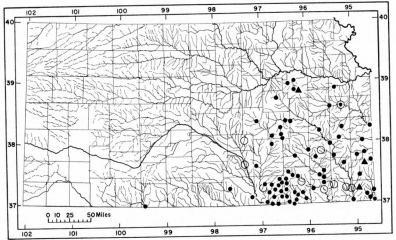

Pomotis auritus, Wheeler (1879:33).

Lepomis megalotis, Cragin (1885b:110); Graham (1885a:4, 1885b:76); Evermann and Fordice (1886:185); Jordan (1891:18); Moore and Buck (1955:26); Schelske (1957:48); Clarke, Breukelman, and Andrews (1958:169); Cross, Deacon, and Ward (1959:163-164); Breukelman (1960:12, 34); Deacon (1961b:398); Kilgore and Rising (1965:242); Metcalf (1966:156).

Lepomis megalotis breviceps, Breukelman (1940b:382); Cross (1954:312); Metcalf (1959:382, 393); Deacon and Metcalf (1961:318).

Lepomis megalotus, Maupin, Wells, and Leist (1954:168, 171).

Lepomis megalotis megalotis, Fisher (1962:428).

Lepomis gibbosus, Cragin (1885b:110).

Eupomotis gibbosus, Dyche (1914:61); Hall (1934:231).

Body highly compressed; dorsal fin usually with 10 spines, 11 soft-rays; anal fin with 3 spines, 9 or 10 soft-rays; pelvics with 1 spine, 5 soft-rays; pectoral fin short and rounded, with 13 rays; lateral-line complete, arched anteriorly, with 35-38 scales; opercular flap long and flexible, slightly decumbent posteriorly; gill rakers short, knoblike; vertebrae 29-31.

Olivaceous dorsally, breast and belly dull orange; young almost uniformly olivaceous, lacking distinct vertical bars; breeding males variegated laterally by brilliantly iridescent green (or turquoise) and orange (or amber) pigment; no discrete orange spots on sides; nape rufous; fins reddish-brown; head with alternating orange and blue-green, vermiform bands laterally; opercular flap iridescent green in life (black in preserved specimens), narrowly bordered by white pigment. See Plate 3.

Maximum length approximately five inches.

The longear is abundant in the eastern part of the Arkansas River System, where it inhabits upland streams having numerous pools, permanent or semi-permanent flow of clear water, and unsilted bottoms of stone or firm clay. Elsewhere, the extent of the native range of *L. megalotis* in Kansas is uncertain, and some early records of sunfishes that I refer to this species are questionable (see synonymy above).

I think that all Kansas records of the pumpkinseed, *L. gibbosus* (Linnaeus), are assignable to *L. megalotis*. The longear is still called "pumpkinseed" by many anglers in Kansas; this misnomer may account for early reports of *gibbosus* from the State. Cragin (1885:110) was first to mention *gibbosus* in Kansas, but his listing of it was on authority of Wheeler, who had previously reported *L. auritus* but not *gibbosus* in the Marais des Cygnes River at Ottawa (Wheeler, 1879:33). *L. auritus* (Linnaeus) certainly is not native to Kansas, but that species resembles *L. megalotis*. Other authors who have mentioned *gibbosus* in Kansas have cited Cragin without adding confirmatory evidence, or have omitted *megalotis* in reporting *gibbosus* from places where *megalotis* occurs. The fish illustrated by Dyche (1914:61) is *L. gibbosus,* but that drawing was taken from Jordan and Evermann (1900: Fig. 429) and is based on a specimen from Wisconsin.

An historical appraisal of records of *L. megalotis* in the Kansas River Basin suggests that the longear has become established in that drainage quite recently. Graham (1885a and 1885b) indicated that the species was found in "Neosho river branches," excluding the Kansas River by implication. No publication prior to 1900 reported longears from drainages other than the Arkansas River in

Kansas, and all specimens obtained by personnel of the State Biological Survey, through 1912, are from the Arkansas Basin. To my knowledge, a specimen obtained in 1951 from Rock Creek, Douglas County, represents the earliest definite record of *megalotis* from the Kansas River System. Longears are abundant now (1966) in Mill Creek and its tributaries in Wabaunsee County. But, as recently as 1953, Mr. James W. Booth found this species at only two of 22 localities where he seined in the Mill Creek Drainage. Those two localities were Lake Wabaunsee, an impoundment on the headwaters of one branch of Mill Creek, and a small brook that flows into the lake. Longears may have been introduced into Lake Wabaunsee from tributaries of the Neosho River that originate less than five miles from that lake. *L. megalotis* has not been reported from other clear, gravelly tributaries of the Kansas River west of the Mill Creek System, or from streams in the Flint Hills north of the Kansas River.

On the other hand, *L. megalotis* almost certainly is indigenous elsewhere in the Missouri River Basin, and may persist in Mill Creek as a relic—as do several other members of the unusually rich fauna of that stream. *L. megalotis* long has occurred abundantly in southern tributaries of the Missouri River in Missouri, including most of the lower Osage River System. Among the records plotted on the map above, the only one that I think definitely results from an introduction is that in Bluff Creek, Comanche County (see Kilgore and Rising, 1965:142).

The longear is caught often by fly-fishermen in streams of southeastern Kansas, but never grows large enough to qualify as an important sport-fish. The average standard lengths of 50 longears from various Kansas streams are as follows, at the ages indicated by Roman numerals: I—2.5 inches; II—2.9 inches; III—3.3 inches; IV—4.3 inches.

The reproductive period of longears in Kansas is long. Specimens in breeding-condition have been found from early May, when water-temperatures were 75° to 85° F., to late July, when temperatures were as high as 87° F. The spawning habits of *L. megalotis* in Missouri have been described by Witt and Marzolf (1954). The home range and movements of longears in streams of Indiana and Louisiana have been discussed by Gunning (1959) and Gunning and Shoop (1963).

Rock bass

Ambloplites rupestris (Rafinesque)

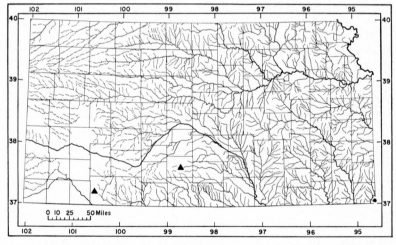

Ambloplites aeneus, Snow (1875:140).
Ambloplites rupestris, Cragin (1885b:110); Graham (1885b:75); Dyche (1914:44); Clarke, Breukelman, and Andrews (1958:169); Breukelman (1960:34); Metcalf (1966:157).

Body compressed; head and mouth large; supramaxilla well-developed; dorsal fin with 11 spines and 11 or 12 soft-rays; anal fin with 5 or 6 spines, 11 soft-rays; pelvics with 1 spine, 5 soft-rays; pectorals short and rounded, with 14 rays; lateral line complete, arched anteriorly, with 40-46 scales; opercle stiff (excluding membrane), slightly *notched* rather than prolonged beyond its small posterior spot; gill rakers slender; vertebrae 31.

Coloration dark, brown to black; sides having scattered dark spots on individual scales, or longitudinally lined by spots; underside of head and breast densely pigmented; fin-membranes (except pectorals) generally dark or heavily spotted; iris red. Young having sides boldly blotched by large dark areas, irregular in outline.

I have found rock bass only in Shoal Creek, Cherokee County, near the locality where Gilbert (1889:42) reported the species in Indian Territory. But, a few rock bass are retained in ponds and aquaria of the Kansas Forestry, Fish and Game Commission at Pratt. Mr. Seth Way, fish-culturist, told me that this species sometimes reproduces in rearing-ponds at Pratt and at Meade County State Park; the young have been stocked in spring-fed impoundments in various parts of Kansas.

The distribution of rock bass at the time of settlement in Kansas cannot be ascertained, but the paucity of early records indicates rarity of the species—if it occurred at all outside the Ozarkian terrain of extreme southeastern Kansas. Snow's (1875:140) record includes a brief color-description that seems applicable only to *A. rupestris,* together with the statement, "rare in the main [Kansas] river but not uncommon in its tributaries." But, Snow failed to include the green sunfish (*Lepomis cyanellus*) in his list, and that species must have been abundant then, as now, in streams near Lawrence. Cragin's report (1885b:110) merely cites Snow, and Graham (1885b:75) listed the rock bass without reference to any locality of occurrence. The report of *Ambloplites* in Lyon County by Clarke, Breukelman, and Andrews (1958:169) is unsupported by definite localities or specimens; though probably valid, this record may result from recent introductions. Breukelman (1960: 12) noted that the rock bass is "found chiefly in the eastern part of the state and seems to be decreasing." I suspect that rock bass formerly occurred farther upstream in the Neosho System than at present, but I doubt that *Ambloplites* inhabited the Kansas River System within historic time. In Missouri, rock bass are restricted to streams of the Ozark Upland, where they are common.

Rock bass prefer clear streams that have a rocky bottom; they usually occupy pools, where they stay near shore or adjacent to boulders, ledges, fallen timber, or other cover. The food of rock bass consists of insects, crustaceans, mollusks, and small fishes. Reproduction occurs in spring, when the males construct and guard nests on gravel-bottom in streams. Rock bass are good sport-fish that commonly attain weights of a pound or more. The species is most vulnerable to live bait.

18—6169

White crappie
Pomoxis annularis Rafinesque

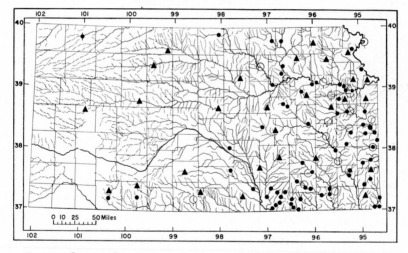

Pomoxys hexacanthus, Snow (1875:140); Wheeler (1879:33).

Pomoxys annularis, Jordan and Meek (1885:14); Cragin (1885b:110); Graham (1885b:75); Gilbert (1886:211); Dyche (1914:52, 54, 55).

Pomoxis annularis, Hall (1934:231); Breukelman (1940a:374, 1940b:382, 1960:12, 34); Jennings (1942:366); Greer and Cross (1956:361); Schelske (1957:48); Clarke, Breukelman, and Andrews (1958:169); Cross, Deacon and Ward (1959:163-164); Metcalf (1959:380-381, 1966:157); Minckley (1959:429); Deacon (1961:399); Deacon and Metcalf (1961:318); Hastings and Cross (1962:8,17).

White crappie—Schoonover and Thompson (1954:174-175).

Body compressed; head small, with abrupt flexure in profile at occiput; mouth large, oblique; supramaxilla well-developed; dorsal and anal fins large and rounded; length of dorsal fin-base much less than distance from dorsal origin to eye; dorsal fin with 5 or 6 spines, 13-15 soft-rays; anal fin with 5 or 6 spines, 17 or 18 soft-rays; pelvic fin with 1 spine, 5 soft-rays; pectoral fins rounded, with 14 rays; lateral line complete, arched anteriorly, with 38-45 scales; vertebrae usually 32 or 33.

Olivaceous dorsally, silvery laterally; upper sides often marked by several (10 or fewer) vague, dark vertical bars; dorsal, caudal, and anal fins marbled by pigment; pelvics and pectorals usually colorless. Breeding males dark, sides of head and breast nearly black, pelvic fins dark.

Largest Kansas specimen 17½ inches long, weight 4 pounds, ¼ ounce [State record for the species, see Kansas Fish and Game 21(3):15; caught by Mr. Frank Miller in a farm pond near Eureka, Greenwood County, on March 30, 1964.]

The white crappie is one of the commonest fishes in Kansas. Recent construction and stocking of lakes and ponds throughout the State undoubtedly have increased the abundance and distribution of this species, but collections by personnel of the State Biological Survey in the 1890's and in 1910-1912 attest that *P. annularis* occurred generally in rivers of eastern Kansas before their impoundment. Many white crappie still are caught in streams, but their importance to anglers is minor compared to that in the newer artificial lakes. White crappie may be unexcelled by any other Kansas fish in terms of the total number caught and their acceptability to anglers. On an April evening in Fall River Reservoir in 1953, three anglers creeled 250 pounds of crappie—an exceptional catch, to be sure, and one that would not now be legal; but, it is a catch indicative of the prevalence of crappie in some impoundments, and the vulnerability of crappie to hook-and-line.

Despite its important contribution to the State's recreational fishery, the white crappie causes problems in fishery-management.

White crappie require live food. The young eat microcrustacea and other zooplankters, whereas adults that are more than six inches long prefer small fish. White crappie can, and often do, subsist solely on microcrustacea, but seldom grow large on that diet alone. In Kansas most crappie live no longer than three or four years. A few survive for six or more years, but in all Kansas lakes that I have checked, two- and three-year-old crappie outnumber four- and five-year-old crappie by more than 20 to 1.

White crappie enter the angling catch at a length of five or six inches, but few fishermen are satisfied with crappie so small; therefore, the angling effort and the harvest are substantial only where numerous crappie eight or more inches long can be caught. Because of their short life-span, crappie must become seven or eight inches long at age 3 or the catch will be poor, regardless of the number of small crappie in a lake. From the angler's standpoint, the total population of crappie is unimportant, except as it affects the number of individuals that grow large enough to be useful to him.

A pair of white crappie can produce 3000 or more young each year. The most fertile acre of water in Kansas cannot produce enough food for crappie to raise one-fifth that number to large size. Therefore, high mortality among the young—due to predation, injury, or disease—is essential to angling-success. Seldom is juvenile mortality excessive in crappie-populations; more often, too many small fish survive, and deplete their food-supply before attaining a size acceptable to anglers. Such "stunting" can occur in large lakes as well as small ones but is more likely to take place in the latter. Large lakes usually have a more complex array of factors that serve to check the abundance of individual species (a more diverse assemblage of predators, for example) than do small lakes. Similarly, large lakes provide a wider variety of food-organisms for each species, reducing the likelihood of their simultaneous depletion. Knowledge of these relationships causes most conservation agencies to advise against stocking of white crappie in farm-ponds; in them, eventual "stunting" of crappie is the rule rather than the exception.

Thus, the white crappie has a paradoxical place in fishery-management. It is a supremely palatable fish, is readily caught, and is capable of sustaining a heavy fishing-pressure. On the other hand, the size normally attained by the species is marginal in terms of angling acceptability. The average weight of crappie caught from most lakes in Kansas is one-third of a pound or less. A slight increase in the abundance of crappie, or reduction in their food-supply, causes the average size to decline enough that anglers cease to harvest them; under these circumstances, this species becomes a liability rather than an asset in its effect on the recreational fishery. No simple means of regulating crappie-populations, to maintain them at levels most favorable for angling, have been discovered. When crappie become stunted, the anglers have a choice of 1) waiting indefinitely for natural reduction of the number, or 2) eradicating the entire fish-population and starting anew. The second solution usually is the more successful.

Black crappie
Pomoxis nigromaculatus (LeSueur)

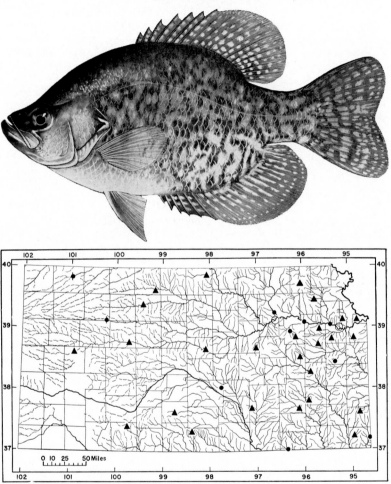

Pomoxys sparoides, Cragin (1885b:110); Dyche (1914:53, 55-57).

Pomoxis sparoides, Hall (1934:231); Breukelman (1940b:382).

Pomoxis nigro-maculatus, Breukelman (1940a:374); Jennings (1942:366).

Pomoxis nigromaculatus, Clarke, Breukelman, and Andrews (1958:169); Cross, Deacon, and Ward (1959:163-164); Metcalf (1959:381, 1966: 158); Minckley (1959:429-430); Breukelman (1960:12,34); Deacon (1961b:399); Deacon and Metcalf (1961:318); Hastings and Cross 1962:8, 16-17).

Black crappie—Schoonover and Thompson (1954:175).

Body compressed; head small, dorsal profile abruptly flexed at occiput; mouth strongly oblique, large, supramaxilla well-developed; dorsal and anal fins large, rounded; length of dorsal-fin base equal to or greater than distance from dorsal origin to eye; dorsal fin with 7 or 8 spines, 15 or 16 soft-rays; anal fin with 6 spines and 18 soft-rays; pelvics with 1 spine, 5 soft-rays; pectorals rounded with 14 rays; lateral line complete, arched anteriorly, with 38-44 scales; vertebrae usually 32 or 33.

Olivaceous or gray-green dorsally; sides having many scattered dark flecks, never arranged in vertical bars; dorsal, caudal and anal fins marbled by pigment, often mainly dark with clear oval spots or "windows." Breeding males with pigment intensified, head and breast black.

Largest Kansas specimen 4 pounds 10 ounces, 22 inches in total length [State record for the species, see Kansas Fish and Game, 23(1):11, 13; caught by Mrs. Hazel Fey of Toronto in Woodson County State Lake].

As indicated by Metcalf (1966:158), the black crappie may not be native to Kansas. Prior to 1900 the only published report of the species was that of Cragin (1885b:110), who credited the record to Wheeler; but, Wheeler (1879) did not include this species in his list of fishes found in the Osage River at Ottawa.

The next writer to mention black crappie in Kansas was Dyche, who stated (1914:56-57), "The crappies that the author caught in Kansas some forty years ago were, as he remembers them, of the white variety. All specimens collected some thirty years ago and preserved for the State University Museum are of the light-colored or white species. The first Black crappies that the author remembers having seen in Kansas were taken at Lake View [an oxbow of Kansas River 5 miles northwest of Lawrence], being propagated from stock that the United States Fish Commission car planted there nearly twenty years ago." Dyche thought that black crappie were displacing white crappie by 1914, "not only at Lake View but apparently in many localities" (op. cit.:60). The oldest specimen of P. nigromaculatus now extant in the University of Kansas collections was taken in 1909, from "old Kaw River beds" one mile north of Lawrence.

Crappie (presumably both species) were produced and distributed by the State Hatchery at Pratt prior to the time of Dyche's commentary, and their propagation has continued to date. Through most of these years, no record distinguished the kind (P. annularis or P. nigromaculatus) that was stocked at particular localities. Most or all crappie currently produced at Pratt are nigromaculatus, and these are stocked exclusively in new impoundments.

Dyche's belief that nigromaculatus often replaced annularis is not borne out by the collections of the State Biological Survey in the 1950's and 1960's. The black crappie is rare in streams of the State, and seldom exceeds P. annularis in abundance in lakes.

Perches

FAMILY PERCIDAE

KEY

1. Preopercle saw-edged; 7 or 8 branchiostegal rays 2
   Preopercle smooth-edged; 5 or 6 branchiostegal rays 4
2. Jaws with strong canine teeth; anal soft-rays 12 or 13; body lacking
   distinct vertical bars of color in adults 3
   Jaws without canine teeth; anal soft-rays 6-8; body having series of
   vertical bars over yellow ground-color,
   yellow perch, Perca flavescens, p. 287
3. Cheeks well scaled; dorsal soft-rays 17-19; spinous dorsal fin spattered
   with distinct black spots, without large dark blotch at posterior base
   of fin; lower lobe of caudal fin not white-tipped,
   sauger, Stizostedion canadense, p. 285
   Cheeks sparsely scaled; dorsal soft-rays 19-22; spinous dorsal fin without distinct dark spots, but with large dark blotch at posterior base;
   lower lobe of caudal fin white-tipped,
   walleye, Stizostedion vitreum, p. 282
4. Belly naked or with median row of enlarged spiny scales (one such
   scale usually present between pelvic fins); anal fin about as large
   as soft-dorsal fin; pelvic fins separated by space about as wide as
   base of each pelvic fin; lateral line complete (see Fig. 20A) . . . 5
   Belly usually covered with ordinary scales (sometimes partly naked,
   but never with enlarged spiny scales on midline or between pelvic
   fins); anal fin usually smaller than soft-dorsal fin; space between
   pelvic fins less than length of fin-base; lateral line complete or incomplete (see Fig. 20B) 10
5. Snout having conical protuberance projecting forward beyond mouth;
   lateral-line scales usually more than 80; sides with alternately long
   and short vertical bars, interrupted ventrally; large dark spot at base
   of caudal fin . . . . logperch, Percina caprodes, p. 293
   Snout not protruding, jaws terminal or nearly so; lateral-line scales
   fewer than 80; color not as above 6

Fig. 20. Differences in scales on the belly and in bases of the pelvic fins in
darters.

A. Belly with a median row of modified scales that are sometimes lost, leaving
a naked strip; pelvic fins separated by a space about as wide as the basal
length of each pelvic fin (genus Percina).

B. Belly with scales like those on sides (sometimes partly naked anteriorly, but
never with a median scaleless strip); pelvic fins separated by a space less
than the basal length of each fin (genus Etheostoma).

6. Greatest depth of body less than ⅐ standard length; anal fin with
single spine .... western sand darter, *Ammocrypta clara*, p. 298
Greatest depth of body more than ⅐ standard length; anal fin with
2 spines 7

7. Groove separating upper jaw from front of head interrupted at tip of
snout, bridged by narrow band of tissue (premaxillaries nonpro-
tractile, Fig. 4); lateral-line scales more than 65 8
Groove separating upper jaw from front of head continuous across tip
of snout (premaxillaries protractile as in Fig. 4, sometimes finely
bridged to snout in *Percina shumardi*); lateral-line scales fewer
than 65 9

8. Gill membranes broadly connected at mid-ventral line, their juncture
nearer base of pelvic fins than tip of lower jaw; spinous dorsal fin
with orange submarginal bar; sides plain dark-colored or blotched
(blotches, if present, more than 8 and vertically elongate),
slender-headed darter, *Percina phoxocephala*, p. 291
Gill membranes separate, their juncture nearer tip of lower jaw than
base of pelvic fins; spinous dorsal fin without orange bar; 7 or 8
horizontally elongate dark blotches on mid-sides,
black-sided darter, *Percina maculata*, p. 289

9. Gill membranes connected, their juncture nearer base of pelvic fins
than tip of snout; cheeks scaly; prominent dark bar below eye; sides
with diffuse, vertically elongate blotches,
river darter, *Percina shumardi*, p. 295
Gill membranes separate, their juncture nearer tip of snout than base
of pelvic fins; cheeks usually naked or with embedded scales (sometimes scaly); no dark bar below eye; mid-sides with line of narrowly connected small dark spots, upper sides having irregular pat-
tern of dark checks .... channel darter, *Percina copelandi*, p. 296

10. Premaxillaries protractile (groove, separating upper jaw from front of
head, continuous across snout; see Fig. 4) 11
Premaxillaries non-protractile (groove along margin of upper jaw interrupted medially; Fig. 4) 14

11. Anal spines 2; dorsal spines 11-14 12
Anal spine usually 1; dorsal spines usually 9 13

12. Mouth ventral, snout rounded; maxillary adnate to preorbital; lateral
line complete; sides with prominent W-markings, breeding males
green with scattered red dots,
green-sided darter, *Etheostoma blennioides*, p. 306
Mouth terminal, snout acute; maxillary free from preorbital; lateral
line incomplete; sides without W-markings, breeding males with
blue lateral spots and brassy sheen,
speckled darter, *Etheostoma stigmaeum*, p. 303

13. Lateral line complete; dark bridle on snout interrupted at midline,
johnny darter, *Etheostoma nigrum*, p. 299
Lateral line incomplete, terminating near middle of body; dark bridle
continuous from eye to eye across front of snout above upper lip,
blunt-nosed darter, *Etheostoma chlorosomum*, p. 302